A Revelation from God
A Pathway to Light

Dr. Gloria G. Watkins

Kingdom Builders Publications LLC

© 2019 Dr. Gloria G. Watkins
A Revelation from God: A Pathway to Light
Kingdom Builders Publications, LLC

All rights reserved. No part of this book may be reproduced or transmitted in any form or by any means without written permission from the author.

Printed in the USA

ISBN 978-0-578-54090-0 Soft Cover

Authored by
Dr. Gloria G. Watkins

Editor
Lakisha S. Forrester
Kingdom Builders Publications

Cover Design
LoMar Designs

A Revelation from God: A Pathway to Light

This Book Belongs to

DEDICATION

This book is dedicated in loving memory of my husband, the late Reverend Dr. Bobby G. Watkins Sr. My inspiration comes from watching him pastor, teach, preach, and help others as a private investigator. For over thirty years, he worked to leave a legacy for his family.

CONTENTS

DEDICATION iii

CONTENTS v

ACKNOWLEDGMENTS 9

Words of Encouragement 10

Preface 11

Introduction 13

Genesis 20:18 14

Exodus 20:18 16

Leviticus 20:8 18

Numbers 20:18 21

Deuteronomy 20:18 23

Joshua 20:8 24

Judges 20:18 26

Ruth 2:1,8 28

1 Samuel 20:18 30

2 Samuel 20:18 32

1 Kings 20:18 33

2 Kings 20:18 34

1 Chronicles 20:1,8 36

2 Chronicles 20:18 38

Ezra 2:1,18 39

Nehemiah 2:18 41

Esther 2:18 42

Job 20:18 44

Psalm 20:1,8 46

Proverbs 20:18 47

Ecclesiastes 2:18 48

Song of Solomon 2:1,8 49

Isaiah 2:1,8 50

Jeremiah 20:18 51

Lamentations 2:18 53

Ezekiel 20:18 55

Daniel 2:18 56

Hosea 2:18 58

Joel 2:18 60

Amos 2:1,8 61

Obadiah 1:1,8 62

Jonah 2:1,8 64

Micah 2:1,8 65

Nahum 2:1,8 66

Habakkuk 2:1,8 68

Zephaniah 2:1,8 69

Haggai 2:1,8 70

Zechariah 2:1,8 71

Malachi 2:1,8 73

Matthew 20:18 75

Mark 2:18 76

Luke 20:18 77

John 20:18 78

Acts 20:18 79

Romans 2:18 80

1 Corinthians 2:1,8 81

2 Corinthians 2:1,8 82

Galatians 2:1,8 84

Ephesians 2:1,8 85

Philippians 2:18 87

Colossians 2:18 89

1 Thessalonians 2:18 91

2 Thessalonians 2:1,8 92

1 Timothy 2:1,8 94

2 Timothy 2:1,8 96

Titus 2:1,8	97
Philemon 1:8	98
Hebrews 2:1,8	100
James 2:1,8	101
1 Peter 2:1,8	102
2 Peter 2:18	104
1 John 2:18	105
2 John 1:8	106
3 John 1:2,8	108
Jude 1:1,18	109
Revelation 20:1,8	111
Epilogue	113
About the Author	114

ACKNOWLEDGMENTS

I have to start by thanking my sons, Bobby G. Watkins II and Jonathan Watkins, for supporting me in this God-given project. I am extremely thankful to my sisters for all their support and prayers. I also extend my gratitude to Kingdom Builders Publications for trusting me in this project for publishing.

WORDS OF ENCOURAGEMENT

"Let the glory of the Lord rise among you."
Taken from Isaiah 60:1b

No matter where you are in life, transition with no pressure or worries. Find yourself. Bring to light what's in your heart. Expose the real you for miraculous change.

When you know your past, you can make better decisions for your future.

When we don't listen to God, we listen to the voices of others or ourselves. We can't ignore the voice of God or Him. He's the only One who can change our generation.

In the dispensation of grace, repent and change, and do not take baggage into the next generation.

PREFACE

As the people of God, we must live in a manner that addresses and reflects the God of our lives. The God who allows us to live, move, and have our being. God wants to speak to us all the time and in many different ways. This book is about the revelation of Jesus Christ. As the time draws near for Christ's return, we are reminded that we have to use our spiritual ears to hear what the Spirit of the Lord is saying to the church.

Out of divine providence, I believe wherever I decide to go in the Bible and whatever scripture I choose, there will be a Word from the Lord for me. I began writing this book in 2018. Specific scriptures were given to me upon hearing the Holy Spirit. They were used as the basis for my devotions. The leading scriptures, using any numerical combinations of 2-0-1-8, will reveal the glory of the Lord in all 66 books of the Bible.

The entire Bible is necessary so that we can live out the manifestation of His presence. If by chance you encounter something in the Bible you don't understand, El Shaddai, our Almighty God is waiting for you to come to Him so He can give you strength, understanding, and wisdom.

In my own personal journey, I have found that I can reveal myself to Him unashamedly, and He will reveal Himself to me in all of His glorious splendor and wonder. I pray that God gives you revelation and encourages you to write your own devotion to Him.

INTRODUCTION

In God's great design of earth's processes, we saw light turn to darkness and back to light again during the eclipse of August 2017. It could be expressed as a lighted path, even though it lasted about 120 seconds. Isn't it remarkable how God would allow man to pinpoint celestial activity that would darken a world, only to reveal to us that His light can go out to total darkness but will return? Make no mistake; it was a level of trust to acknowledge that it would be light again.

The road of life often takes us traveling down uncharted territory and voyaging through the seas. When the path ahead isn't clearly visible or it's even darkened somehow, we tend to launch out into the deep. God's plan may not always be apparent to us, but He promised to always be with us to the very end of the voyage, regardless of the years, times, and seasons.

GENESIS 20:18

18 For the LORD had closed up all the wombs of the house of Abimelech because of Sarah, Abraham's wife.

Abraham journeyed from the south to a place called Gerar, a Philistine city, with his wife Sarah. He told Abimelech, the king of Gerar, that Sarah was his sister *(Genesis 20:2)*. Sarah joined in her husband's lie to deceive the king. This resulted in Sarah being taken into Abimelech's harem.

This wasn't the first time Abraham used this ploy. He also did so in *Genesis 12:10-20*. We saw that history repeated itself. Although mistakes, half-truths, and lies were told, God protected Sarah's honor. The Lord intervened. He came to Abimelech in a dream to tell him not only is Sarah married, but also he kept him from touching her, which would have resulted in sin. Abimelech earnestly protested his innocence and integrity before the Lord. After all, he was tricked. Demonstrating proper submission and heeding to the warning of the words the Lord spoke, he gave Sarah back to her husband *(Genesis 20:3-6)*.

The deceit of Abraham and Sarah was critical enough to evoke God's personal and dramatic intervention. Sometimes, God steps into our life's situations, although we were the ones who made the mess and straightens things out. He does that because He has a plan that no one can intervene in. You see, Abraham couldn't have fully trusted God for protection in Gerar. Otherwise, why would he have gone through such great lengths attempting to be wise in his own eyes with the deceptive plan? He could have jeopardized the covenant if God did not intervene each time.

Although Abimelech rebuked Abraham's deceitful sinning, he still showed him kindness, grace, and generosity. Lies and deceit can thwart blessings and can sometimes become generational sins. This was repeated in *Genesis 26:9* when Isaac, his child, his son of promise, did the same thing when he introduced his wife Rebekah as his sister to Abimelech. Through the exchanges in Genesis, there were many portraits of grace, forgiveness, submission, trust, and distrust. It is only through salvation and an earnest walk towards modeling biblical principles can we seek God to break the generational curses and heal our families.

God will protect His covenant and His anointing.

EXODUS 20:18

¹⁸ Now all the people witnessed the thunderings, the lightning flashes, the sound of the trumpet, and the mountain smoking.

When the people saw this cluster of phenomena occurring, they trembled, fearfully withdrew, and stood afar off. Accompanying this theophany, with the appearance of God on the mountain, they instinctively placed Moses in position as the mediator between God and themselves. Because such was the gap between Moses and the Holy God, the people feared they were not fit to live in His presence.

Consider this: The tenth commandment is about controlling the desires of the heart. Sinful thoughts beget sinful actions *(Matthew 15:19; James 1:14-15)*. So, it is no surprise that covetous people often break the commandments to satisfy their greed and appetites. A fear of God motivates a desire to both obey and honor Him. Israel lost their reverence for the Lord and became afraid of His presence.

Are you afraid of God's presence? Don't be afraid. God has come to instill a deep and reverent awe in us so that we won't sin. If you find yourself in a space where your world is not so perfect, repent (change). You have an advocate. You are not alone *(1 John 1:9)*. To the non-Christian, you too, need to get to know Jesus as your Savior.

Although we are living in a sinful and dying world, we must remember that every day is a new day. Let's hold on to God's presence and live each day as if it is our last. It is in His presence that we will find the fullness of joy and He will show us the path of life. We have to allow His presence to direct us by staying in the Word and communing in prayer. It is at God's right hand that we will find pleasures forever more *(Psalm 16:11)*.

Don't be afraid of God's presence.

LEVITICUS 20:8

⁸ *And you shall keep My statutes, and perform them: I am the LORD who sanctifies you.*

The interlocking themes in the Book of Leviticus are: (a) holiness, (b) worship, (c) law, (d) presence, and (e) atonement.

Approaching a God is not a casual undertaking. We have to deal with the sins that separate us from Him. Separating from the sin is a sacrifice that we need to make, because there are consequences for sin, which leads to death. Worship is a way to maintain fellowship with the Holy God.

God stressed that His people should do what is right and do it in the right way. There is a wrong way to do the right thing, but never a right way to do the wrong thing. We can't live like everyone else in the world and be called by God's name.

There were obvious penalties for breaking the laws of Israel. Leviticus, was a how-to book for ceremonies and worship practices within the Old Testament system, filled with regulations and ordinances. The Ten Commandments, written on stone, served as an external reminder to the laws of God *(Exodus 24:12)*. God's people have to become internally motivated to live a holy life, by having the laws written in the tablets of their hearts *(Jeremiah 31:33)*.

God is set apart from all other gods, and we must serve Him as the holy and righteous God that He is. He sanctifies and makes His people holy. It was no easy feat for the infant nation of Israel to learn God's ways and become a "set apart people." In fact, they lived their lives with a Holy God in their midst and still made missteps and many wrong turns on the way to the Promised Land. This is true of believers today as well. Even though we have God's spirit living within us, there is a need to be reminded of His nearness and cultivate a sense of His presence. To stay in His presence, scripture urges us to cleanse ourselves of all filthiness of the flesh and spirit, perfecting holiness in the fear of God *(2 Corinthians 7:1)*. The sure knowledge of God's presence should not only flood our lives with comfort, but also fill us with a healthy dread of not wanting to offend Him or cause His Spirit to grieve.

God's willingness to dwell in the midst of sinful people was a sign of His grace and forgiveness. It also foretold of the future when God's presence would dwell in the tabernacle among humanity in human flesh, and later in human hearts *(Matthew 5:8; John 1:14; Hebrews 10:22)*.

We have to atone for our mistakes, which means to make amends for a wrong that was done. The word atonement can be found 51 times in the Book of Leviticus. In that day, they used to offer up animals as their sin offering. This practice would be replaced when the perfect Lamb of God paid the ultimate and final sacrifice of Himself for all *(Hebrews 9:1-15, 24-28; Hebrews 10:1-14)*. We only have to offer our own lives unto God.

Listen to the Lord's still small voice as He tells us that He has separated us and we must not live like the nations He has casted out before us. There are penalties for breaking God's law and following after pagan perversions. We have to accept the fact, as people of God, we are held to a higher standard.

God is our best example of holiness.
1 Peter 1:16

NUMBERS 20:18

18 Then Edom said to him, "You shall not pass through my land, lest I come out against you with the sword."

Edom is mentioned approximately 125 times in the Old Testament. Many of the references pertain to prophetic judgment, partly because of the king of Edom's decision on one night while Moses was at a crossroads at Kadesh. Moses was leading the people of Israel and he wanted to take them through Edom on the way to the Promised Land through the King's highway. He requested permission to enter through the land. It was a reasonable request, a much easier route to pass through, to be exact. However, the king refused their entrance. His refusal historically changed the destiny of millions of people and their livestock, thus, erasing the hopes of a whole generation.

From reading about Moses and his experiences, I have learned that it is never wise to get in the path God wants to take His people. God's way was the highway and Edom's refusal of allowing them access through this vantage point led to a fall in humanity.

Previously, in this chapter, there was mentioning of a lack of water. To solve this problem, God instructed Moses to speak to the rock in the desert, so the water would flow through it and the land and people would no longer thirst. Unfortunately, Moses angrily struck the rock instead. His act of disobedience was not without consequence. As a result, God did not allow him to lead Israel into Canaan, the Promised Land.

I have often wondered why Moses was obedient in Exodus 17:6 when God asked him to strike the rock at Horeb, but he decided to disobey in Numbers when he was asked only to speak to the rock. I have also wondered why God didn't just let them go into the Promised Land, considering they had been through so much.

However, I am reminded that God must be obeyed. When He tells us to do something, it is for our good. Veering from His instructions will only cause of unnecessary heartache and trouble, which was evident in the story of Adam and Eve. I am thankful that the promises of God are not invalidated by the failures of humanity. Whatever He says and speak, so it will be done.

When God sets destiny in motion, humanity can't stop it.

DEUTERONOMY 20:18

18 Lest they teach you to do according to all their abominations which they have done for their gods, and you sin against the LORD your God.

Being amongst heathen nations could ultimately cause sinful corruption. The Canaanite cities represented wickedness. Because Israel was chosen to bear witness of the one and true living God, the Lord ordered them to destroy those cities so they wouldn't influence them to sin.

Excommunicate yourselves from carriers of sin. Eliminate any sinful influences or as the Hebrews put it, anything that so easily besets us from running God's race. Test your spirit, soul, and body; and put them in check.

The Book of Deuteronomy reveals much about the attributes of God. It teaches us that the Lord is the only God and that He is jealous and faithful, merciful and loving, yet angered by sin. God called Israel and present-day believers to obey, fear, love, and serve Him by walking in His ways and keeping His commandments. By obeying God, the people would receive His blessing *(Deuteronomy 28:1-14)*. Obedience and the pursuit of holiness are always based upon the character of God. Because of who He is; His people are to be holy.

It costs to sin against God.

JOSHUA 20:8

⁸ And on the other side of the Jordan, by Jericho eastward, they assigned Bezer in the wilderness on the plain, from the tribe of Reuben, Ramoth in Gilead, from the tribe of Gad, and Golan in Bashan, from the tribe of Manasseh.

Moses designated six cities of refuge. People who accidently or inadvertently killed another could flee to any of those cities for protection. If God made provision for the presumed innocent or guilty to be protected while awaiting trial, how much more is He a refuge for His children?

God is our refuge *(Deuteronomy 33:27)* and our strength *(Psalm 46:10)* in the times of trouble *(Psalm 9:9)* and in times of distress *(Jeremiah 16:19)*.

I'm sure at some point you have needed refuge (a secret place) because of a mistake, act, or misfortune. Did you cry out to God in hopes that He would hide you in the safety of His arms, so you would not be overtaken by the avenger of blood *(Numbers 35:19, 26-27; Deuteronomy 19:11-12)*? This avenger of blood is the adversary who comes to kill and destroy. But, God comes to give us abundant life. We have to confess, put the issue at His feet, and wait for Him to make provision, because He is our safe haven.

Let God be your secret place.

JUDGES 20:18

^{18} Then the children of Israel arose and went up to the house of God to inquire of God. They said, "Which of us shall go up first to battle against the children of Benjamin?" The LORD said, "Judah first!"

The Levite in the hill country of Ephraim was married to a concubine, a lower status wife—a harlot. She was involved in sexual immorality and deserted him. After four months, despite her sin, he found her and tried to persuade her to return home with him. She took him to her father's house. After the requirement of hospitality (food and shelter) was over, the Levite and his concubine journeyed to Gibeah.

When they arrived to Gibeah, they went to the town's open square where the travelers usually sat. An old man offered them hospitality. The scene of what seemingly was going to be a peaceful hospitality soon turned into a virtual re-enactment of Sodom and Gomorrah by perverted men. They requested that the old man give them the Levite so that they can have sex with him. But he offered them his daughter and the concubine instead. The Levite pushed his concubine into the crowd of violent men.

They raped her all night and at daybreak, they let her go. After that, she went to the old man's house and fell at the door. The Levite picked her up, took her body home, and cut her up in twelve pieces, which he sent to all of the twelve tribes of Israel as an outpour of outrage. Her carved up body achieved remarkable unity between the tribes of Israel. However, the tribe of Benjamin did not take part in the assembly. All the people decided to take a united action with the Israelites and send messengers appealing to the Benjamites to hand over the guilty men. They would not because they were concerned about tribal solidarity, rather than national solidarity or justice.

Consequently, Israel assembled for war at Bethel and inquired of God. God answered and told them to send Judah first. A victory was imminent for Benjamin. God's yes was a progression, not an immediate victory. It took three tries for Israel, with fasting and weeping before God, before He gave them victory. Each time, we must ask and operate according to God's answer. Granted, sometimes defeat can be discouraging; however, elation is always in victory.

> A **Yes** from God equals victory.

RUTH 2:1,8

¹ There was a relative of Naomi's husband, a man of great wealth, of the family of Elimelech. His name was Boaz.

⁸ Then Boaz said to Ruth, "You will listen, my daughter, will you not? Do not go to glean in another field, nor go from here, but stay close to my young women."

During the last days of Israel's judges, an Israelite family moved to the land of Moab to escape a famine in Israel. In Israel's case, there was more than just an absence of food. A spiritual famine arose which led to a physical famine.

Moses had warned the people that if they failed to cleanse the Promised Land of pagan corruption, their fields and flocks would be cursed *(Deuteronomy 28:17-18; 22-24; 38-40)*. When the physical famine fell upon Israel, they sought food in the enemy's territory, the idolatrous Moab.

The Book of Ruth captures the irony of an Israelite family (Elimelech, his wife Naomi, and their two sons) leaving Bethlehem—the house of bread—a symbol of God's fullness—searching for bread in a pagan Moab. Elimelech died, leaving Naomi with their two sons who eventually married women from Moab. Later, when the two sons died, Ruth took her two Moabite daughters-in-law, Ruth and Orpah to Judah, but only Ruth went with her to Bethlehem. It was there in Bethlehem that set the stage for a beautiful story of a redeeming love, loyalty, kindness, faithfulness, marriage, and God's sovereignty.

Boaz, a relative of Naomi's deceased husband, was also a man of distinction and wealth who used his influence and resources to be God's special provision for Ruth. He made sure she had enough by allowing her to take the scraps from his fields. His actions revealed him as a man of pity, prayer, provision, and protection. Ruth cared for Naomi in that same spirit.

Boaz, Naomi, and Ruth were three people who went against status quo and faithfully heeded the Lord's direction, even when they could not see where it would take them. When we start to walk in God's way, He will direct us. He steers our course when we take our hands off the wheel. As we follow His lead, we can trust Him to redeem the hardships of our past and provide for us in the present moment.

The power of a redeeming love.

I SAMUEL 20:18

¹⁸ Then Jonathan said to David, "Tomorrow is the New Moon; and you will be missed, because your seat will be empty."

During the New Moon *(Isaiah 1:14; I Samuel 20:5)*, the first day of the month's civil or religious festival, there was a sacrificial meal of celebration where trumpets blared. David knew Saul would expect his presence at the meal, but he did not want to risk his life, without knowing Saul's true intentions. David was aware that there was an attempt on his life by Saul previously. Saul ordered his son Jonathan and others to kill David.

Jonathan, because he favored David, warned him. He spoke highly of David to his father reminding him of all of David's victorious attributes in battle. Jonathan, trying to be the peacemaker, brought the two before each other. Saul, overcome by an evil spirit, tried to kill David with a spear. Naturally, David escaped.

David's anxiety about attending the celebration was definitely warranted. It was unclear if: (a) Saul would try to take his life again, (b) if they would reconcile, or (c) if David would be considered an outlaw and always having to be on the run in fear of his life.

Jonathan promised to find out his father's intentions regarding the New Moon's celebration. By him denoting his empty seat at the event, David received his answer and fled to a place of safety. Jonathan and David pledged their loyalty to each other and to the covenant. Jonathan transferred his allegiance from his father to David, the future anointed king.

> The Lord's covenant requires loyalty.

2 SAMUEL 20:18

¹⁸ So she spoke, saying, "They used to talk in former times, saying, 'They shall surely seek guidance at Abel,' and so they would end disputes."

Joab's troops overwhelmed Sheba's troops around the perimeter of Abel in Israel and began knocking the wall down. A wise woman told Joab that it was unwise to destroy Israel, which was the inheritance from the Lord and that there was a designated city to settle disputes.

Abel means a fresh grassy and peaceful meadow. It was a city of long standing within the nation that had a reputation as being a place where wisdom often settled disputes. Abel informed her that it was not his intention to destroy Israel; however, Sheba rose up against David. The wise woman agreed to assist Joab in his efforts to throw Sheba's head over the wall *(2 Samuel 20:20)*.

The Lord shepherds, leads, guides, and provides stillness and restoration to our soul.
Psalm 23

---

1 KINGS 20:18

[18] So he said, "If they have come out for peace, take them alive; and if they have come out for war, take them alive."

Ben-hadad, Syria's king, along with his other kings sent a message to Ahab promising to destroy Samaria. A prophet came to Ahab, Israel's king, with divine words of encouragement, assurance, and instructions on how to start the battle. While he and his Israelite troops marched to Syria for the attack, Ben-hadad and his drunken kings found out they were coming. He ordered them, regardless if the Israelites came in peace or war, to take them alive. Ultimately, victory belonged to Ahab. This victory may have looked natural to the enemies, but it was in fact supernatural. Following God's precise instructions will bring about His desired result. Veering to the left or right could be destructive.

Think about how the enemy works when he comes to attack and we are not on our spiritual posts. We have to be ready at all times to combat the schemes of Satan with the Word, knowledge, and belief in God.

God prepares us for victory.

2 KINGS 20:18

[18] 'And they shall take away some of your sons who will descend from you, whom you will beget; and they shall be eunuchs in the palace of the king of Babylon.'

Hezekiah was sick, near death, and told to get his house in order from the Prophet Isaiah. He faced the wall and began to pray to the Lord. He prayed that the Lord finds him to be obedient in all that he was assigned to do and that He considers his heart and actions to be right in His sight.

The Lord heard his petitions and sent Isaiah back to give him a message that He planned to heal him and deliver him from the Assyrian army. The Lord honored His word. When applied, the medicinal properties of the pressed twigs healed Hezekiah. Additionally, the Lord extended his life an additional 15 years.

Because he wanted to impress Babylonia, Hezekiah, a man of great faith, allowed his sin of foolish pride to expose all of Judah's treasures to this embassy *(2 Kings 20:12-13)*. Isaiah returned with a rebuke from the Lord. Essentially, Hezekiah exposed the treasures to the enemy's camp and this led to his downfall. Babylon, under the rule of Nebuchadnezzar, eventually came to Jerusalem to seize these treasures *(2 Kings 24:10-13; 2 Kings 25:11-17)*.

Use wisdom in exposure.

---

1 CHRONICLES 20:1,8

¹ It happened in the spring of the year, at the time kings go out to battle, that Joab led out the armed forces and ravaged the country of the people of Ammon, and came and besieged Rabbah. But David stayed at Jerusalem. And Joab defeated Rabbah and overthrew it.

⁸ These were born to the giant in Gath, and they fell by the hand of David and by the hand of his servants.

The elimination of giants is an important aspect of how David finally took possession of the entire Promised Land. After three battles, a notable giant was killed *(I Samuel 17)*. The defeat of the giant meant that finally the land and the situation had been conquered.

A giant can be anything that causes us to stumble and not walk in the solidarity of God's promises. Giants keep us stagnant—whether they are operating in our surroundings or within our own spirit or mind. We have to kill the giants in our lives or they will perpetually torment or kill us. By kill, I mean not to let them overtake us. We have to uproot every sin that so easily beset us *(Hebrews 12:1)*. Turning our focus back on the Holy Spirit and letting Him guide and rule our lives are instrumental facets in eliminating the giants.

The residue of the giant must go!

---

2 CHRONICLES 20:18

¹⁸ And Jehoshaphat bowed his head with his face to the ground, all Judah and the inhabitants of Jerusalem bowed before the lord, worshiping the LORD.

When the day arrived, Jehoshaphat implemented his usual strategy for battle. He attempted to restructure his kingdom by acknowledging the dominion of the Lord through fasting, prayer, praise, seeking, and trusting God. He appointed those who sang to the Lord to lead the army. In times of battle, thanksgiving can bring about security and deliverance as it did for Jehoshaphat and his troops. Only the Lord of Lords can make the enemies destroy each other, which caused this battle to be victorious. Praise the Lord for his mercy endures forever *(Psalm 107:1)*.

God fights our battles *(2 Chronicles 20:15)*, but that doesn't mean that we don't have a part. We are to dress ourselves in battle attire with truth, righteousness, peace, faith, salvation, prayer, and thanksgiving *(Ephesians 6:14-18)*.

The key to the battle is worship.

EZRA 2:1,18

¹ Now these are the people of the province who came back from captivity, of those who had been carried away, whom Nebuchadnezzar, the king of Babylon had carried away to Babylon, and who returned to Jerusalem and Judah, everyone to his own city.

¹⁸ the people of Jorah, one hundred and twelve

Israel's lack of spiritual discipline and obedience brought God's judgment in the form of captivity. When that happened, the descendants of that generation stood there looking at what spiritual idolatry and apathy produced. While the Jews worked to rebuild the city, would they also rebuild themselves into a nation that honored and worshipped God? One man within the returning nation made it his personal mission to answer yes to that question. His name was Ezra. Ezra, a Levitical priest and scribe, was a spiritual leader who encouraged purification and dependence on God. Purification would result in repentance (a separation and opposition to sin) and restoration of individuals and the community.

Although there were many people who returned from exile, the number 112 intrigued me the most. That number represented the people of Jorah. Consider this: one hundred is a multiple of the numeral ten. It is the beginning of a new series of numbers forming a new cycle. Accordingly, ten denotes the complete perfection of divine order. Not only do we see ten times ten, but add twelve to that and you will get manifested sovereignty in governmental perfection.

Whether you are being held captive in your mind or by circumstances, plan for a new cycle of divine order for success. Many times, you are not directly responsible for your captivity; however, restoration is your responsibility.

Don't just lay down and die. Rise!

NEHEMIAH 2:18

[18] And I told them of the hand of my God which had been good upon me, and also of the king's words he had spoken to me. So they said "Let us rise up and build." Then they set their hands to do this good work.

It is time to change your posture. Look at the political climate. There are wars, rumors of wars, death, and devastation. Arise in as much as it lies within you. Let the hand of our God be good upon you for empowerment.

Arise, shine; For your light has come!
Isaiah 60:1

ESTHER 2:18

18 Then the king made a great feast, the Feast of Esther, for all his officials and servants; and he proclaimed a holiday in the provinces and gave gifts according to the generosity of a king.

In the Book of Esther, we see the divine providence (the "prearrangement") of a sovereign God orchestrating the affairs of humanity through direct and indirect intervention. In other words, in times that God seems to be hidden and we perceive His silence as Him not acting or fighting on our behalf, that is, in fact, not the case at all. He is ever-presently championing for us, even when we may not feel Him or hear His voice.

In the king's feast, there were no limits on how much wine they could drink. Many were left in a drunken stupor, including King Xerxes. In his impaired state, the king wanted to put all his goods on display, including his wife Queen Vashti. He wanted her to wear a crown, which she refused. Her assertion of independence was considered disobedience. She was ultimately banned from ever entering the kingdom again. Through divine providence, Esther became the new queen.

Esther, a beautiful and influential, yet wise woman, was instrumental in interceding in Haman's plot to annihilate her people and Mordecai. Mordecai, her cousin, was from Persia. He raised Esther when her parents died. Essentially, it was a secret that she was Jewish. That information would have been dangerous to expose. However, when she found out about

Haman's plot, she could be silent no more about her true ancestry. She was willing to risk her own life to help her people. Esther knew that prayer and fasting were needed in order to get help.

Esther devised a plan and looked upon Mordecai to carry out her instructions. Everything worked according to plan and Haman's plot was exposed to the king. In addition, Esther exposed her true heritage to her husband. Because of the favor she had with him, he had Haman killed on the very pole that was meant for Mordecai.

The Feast of Esther was held to celebrate the deliverance of the Jews from the hands of Haman. Although not mentioned by name, the story of Esther teaches us that God meticulously guides our footsteps, even when we may be unaware or when things don't seem to make sense. We may have many plans of our own; however, our will cannot triumph God's will for our lives *(Proverbs 16:9)*. As individuals, we are responsible for walking through the Lord's open doors and abandoning the ones He's closed *(Isaiah 22:22; Revelation 3:8)*.

Only God can be invisible and present at the same time.

JOB 20:18

¹⁸ He will restore that for which he has labored, and will not swallow it down; from the proceeds of business He will get no enjoyment.

At the beginning of the Book of Job, it seemed just to be about a crisis and suffering. By the conclusion of Job, we saw God's sovereignty. Zophar, Bildad, and Eliphaz, the friends who came to help Job, were devastated by what was happening to him. Job lost everything—health, family, animals, servants, and possessions *(Job 1:13-22; Job 2:7)*.

What began as comfort from three friends ended up resulting in inaccurate speculations. They began making assumptions that Job's unfortunate experiences had to be a result of his own disobedience, greed, sin, and wickedness. To them, God was a fair God and wouldn't inflict this kind of harm or punishment without just cause. As you can see, Job's support system wasn't so supportive. They only contributed to more tears, anguish, anxiety, and depression. They encouraged him to confess and repent, so he could get the blessings of God back. Yet, their assertions were all incorrect. The Lord rejected their claims. The Lord corrected them regarding the situation and His own character *(Job 38:2)*. God's anger turned towards them. Job's friends discovered that he wasn't wicked at all, but was a faithful and righteous man. God told them to offer a burnt sacrifice of seven rams and seven bulls to Job *(Job 42:7-9)*. The Lord promised not to bring wrath against them once Job prayed for them. Job did so, and the Lord honored His word, thus, restoring treasures unto Job. He received more abundant blessings at the end of his suffering, than he had at the beginning *(Job 42:12; Joel 2:25)*.

This suffering also taught Job not to question the Lord and that His plans and thoughts are strategic for a desired purpose that will work out in the end. In the Old Covenant, sin and suffering were connected because of their nature. It was believed that keeping God's statutes resulted in blessings, whereas not keeping them resulted in cursing *(Leviticus 26; Deuteronomy 28)*. We see in this matter that being faithful and righteous does not exempt any of us from experiencing suffering.

Satan (the third party) was allowed to operate and cause Job great harm. God granted Satan permission to sift Job as wheat in any aspect; however, the only stipulation was that he was not allowed to take his life. In all suffering, there is a Godly purpose. Trials come from three reasons: (a) unaddressed sin, (b) to increase your faith, and (c) give you a deeper or more accurate knowledge of God. As we learned from Job, suffering is not always a result of our direct actions. It's easy to perceive the suffering of yourself and others wrong. We have to stand firm in the truth of God. God can use anything for His glory and to mature us in Him. The Lord restored Job and He can restore us too.

God can use suffering for our good.
Genesis 50:20

PSALM 20:1,8

¹ *May the LORD answer you in the day of trouble; May the name of the God of Jacob defend you.*

⁸ *They have bowed down and fallen; but we have risen and stand upright.*

Preparation for battle is necessary, but trust in God should be our number one priority. The name of the Lord refers to His character, reputation, and nature.

David gained confidence as he meditated on his God and saw victories through supernatural means.

The Lord answers in the day of trouble.

PROVERBS 20:18

¹⁸ Plans are established by counsel; by wise counsel wage war.

The plans for our lives are established, arranged, and purposed by God through His divine power. *Jeremiah 29:11* declares that the Lord is in full control. Nothing escapes or surprises Him. He is the divine orchestrator of our lives and in Him, we can fully trust.

We have to be in relationship with Him to get the full manifestation of His glory. Wisdom is what we need. If we ask for it, He is faithful to give it to us (*James 1:5*). Being wise in our own eyes leads to downfalls, pits, and obstacles.

Do not wage war on good counsel, which demonstrates a lack of wisdom. God can direct our paths and allow us to make effective decisions for success. Victory is ours when we commit our lives to Him.

God can do what seems to be the impossible.

ECCLESIASTES 2:18

18 Then I hated all my labor in which I had toiled under the sun, because I must leave it to the man who will come after me.

Those who think their ultimate eternity is in the accomplishment of life will be disappointed. No matter how carefully you manage your riches, you cannot control what the person who comes after you will do with those riches.

As believers, we must be careful not to slip into the mindset of evaluating life on what has been accumulated. Instead, we must seek His instructions and set our affections on things above (*Psalm 49:10; Colossians 3:1-2*).

Accomplishment is not the ultimate eternity.

SONG OF SOLOMON 2:1,8

¹ I am the rose of Sharon, and the lily of the valleys.

⁸ The voice of my beloved! Behold, he comes leaping upon the mountains, skipping upon the hills.

The rose of Sharon is a wild autumn flower and the lily of the valley is a delicate white blossom associated with weddings. This book celebrates the love of Solomon and his bride, who is referred to as the Shulamite. The Shulamite was a rarity. She exemplified the beauty, essence, and mystique of those flowers.

The excitement of their courtship, the beauty of the wedding night, the first and subsequent nights, as well as the tender friendships, are all of the elements that make this book a celebration of romance and conjugal love as God intended to be in marriage. This couple began a habit of admiration and affirmation that would be of benefit throughout their marriage.

Song of Solomon also teaches that there is a right time for fulfilling sexual desire (Verse 7). They have found each other and Solomon rejoices in the entitlement of her love.

Celebrate love in marriage.

ISAIAH 2:1,8

¹ The word that Isaiah the son of Amoz saw concerning Judah and Jerusalem.

⁸ Their land is also full of idols; they worship the work of their own hands, that which their own fingers have made.

The Prophet Isaiah accused God's people of sin and rebelling against the one who made them and redeemed them. His message was relatively simply: He instructed them to reform their ways and act obediently. Isaiah announced God's judgment on the people because of their sin.

Unfortunately, many of them chose to delve into idolatry, which signifies a root of evil. In this text, the idols were manmade images or objects. Paul alluded to these images in *Romans 1:23* as he referred to the folly of exchanging the glory of an incorruptible and honorable God into an image resembling a corruptible man and/or animals. God also revealed his future restoration of the people, or at least the faithful remnant that survived the judgment.

As we examine the increasing uses of technology, the innovation of communicating through and/or locating information can become quite addictive. For many, devices such as cell phones and computers have become idols. Imagine the time that is spent on those information highways on a daily basis versus the amount of time spent seeking the face and heart of the Lord. Anything or anyone that we put above the Lord can become an idol if we're not careful.

Expose sin and reform.

JEREMIAH 20:18

¹⁸ Why did I come forth from the womb to see labor and sorrow, that my days should be consumed with shame?

Jeremiah endured much criticism. He struggled inwardly but never wavered in fulfilling his mission. His wish that he had never been born was reminiscent of Job cursing the day of his own birth because of intense suffering *(Job 3:1)*.

Some of the greatest saints in history have suffered from moments of despair, depression, affliction, and wanted to give up *(I Kings 19:4)*. Jeremiah's wish that he had never come forth from his mother's womb is a reminder that the Lord's call is never a guarantee of an easy life *(Lamentations 3:1)*. Be encouraged. You are here for a planned purpose *(Ephesians 2:10)*.

You can do it!

LAMENTATIONS 2:18

¹⁸ Their heart cried out to the Lord, "O wall of the daughter of Zion, let tears run down like a river day and night; Give yourself no relief; give your eyes no rest."

The pagan nations made insulting gestures at Jerusalem, the city that was the perfection of beauty (*Psalm 50:2*) and the joy of the whole earth. It was now an object of ridicule. The Lord brought forth punishment through judgment. However, despite the enemy gloating over Judah, its destruction was not ultimately due to his cunning power. It was merely God's plan.

The wall's ability to cry and produce tears like people is an example of personification. The tears would continue to flow as long as the ruins remained. There was violence, desperation, sorrow, and immense suffering among the people.

Although knee-deep in the worst situation imaginable, a reviving thought of hope gripped the prophet's mind. He focused on the Lord's mercy, compassion, and faithfulness. *Jeremiah 3:21* gives us hope that the Lord hears our cries. As a believer, when circumstances seek to crush us, we must deepen our faith, rely on the Lord, and rise above the tribulations with the Word.

There is a penalty for sin.

EZEKIEL 20:18

[18] But I said to their children in the wilderness, do not walk in the statutes of your fathers, nor observe their judgments, nor defile yourselves with their idols.

God commanded that they live according to His statutes. He was very specific on how they were to maintain themselves in integrity and purity, so they would not be overtaken by defilement.

We have the Bible as our guide. It shows us how to walk upright in the Lord. Imagine the times we have fallen short even after salvation. In Isaiah 48:9, the Lord chose not to destroy for the sake of His name. We should be thankful that not all of our disobedience ends up in punishment. God is faithful to forgive us if we repent and choose to follow His ways. It is for the sake of God that we exist.

Have you ever questioned why are you still here?

DANIEL 2:18

¹⁸ That they might seek mercies from the God of heaven concerning this secret, so that Daniel and his companions might not perish with the rest of the wise men of Babylon.

The theme for the book of Daniel is: "Hope for the people of God during the time of the Gentiles." This time span occurred between Babylonian's captivity and the return of Christ. It was a time when God's people lived under the dominion of an ungodly world.

Despite the uncertainty of the world around him, Daniel was patient, as impulsiveness is not of the Lord. Impulsive people generally forge ahead with their own perspectives and answers, rather than waiting for God's response.

Daniel's actions to seek God, the divine revelator who lives on the inside of us, for the secret (interpretation) of King Nebuchadnezzar's dream illustrated how a great leader should handle crisis in an ungodly situation. He spoke with sound counsel and deep wisdom to the authorities and asked the king to give him time so that he and his friends might seek God concerning this secret. He understood that only through divine revelation could the dream's meaning be uncovered and that he needed to spend time in prayer.

> The Most High God is in control.
> **Daniel 5:21**

HOSEA 2:18

¹⁸ In that day I will make a covenant for them with the beasts of the field, with birds of the air, and with creeping things of the ground. Bow and sword of battle I will shatter from the earth, to make them lie down safely.

Little is known about Hosea the man, but we learned quickly from his character that he was faithful and obedient in spite of the circumstances. God gave Hosea a shocking assignment. He told him to find and marry a harlot and produce children with her (*Hosea 1:2-3*). He did as the Lord asked. In fact, the Lord named the children for them.

Because of anger, unfaithfulness, unwillingness, a lack of compassion, and unforgiveness on a short-term or long-term basis, we can easily miss the assignment God has for us and single-handedly destroy our own destiny. This can cause us to drift away from Him.

God considered Israel to be an adulterous people. The people began to seek everything except God, and pull away from His sovereignty. Israel was tempted, attracted, and intrigued by gods other than the true living God. Because Israel's attention, love, focus, and affections were diverted from God, its people began having an affair with the world. This was going on before they even entered the Promised Land.

Moses warned them to hold fast and hang on to God with everything in them. However, their lusts for other gods drew them away. Jesus told us to take heed, watch, and pray (*Mark*

13:33). If you get too comfortable and lax on studying, praying, and meditating on the Word, it may become easy for you to slip into idolatry. We have to stay vigilant, because even releasing the grip of the Word in just a small dose can become dangerous to our purpose.

Although God is sovereign, we are always under Satan's radar. He is watching and waiting for us to drift little by little into a disaster so that he can draw us away from Christ. We are more susceptible in letting this happen when we allow our interests and preoccupations to replace our pursuit of Christ. When we replace God, we become spiritual adulterers, like the people of Israel.

If you ever find yourself in spiritual adultery, torn between two lovers (Christ and the world) *(Matthew 6:24)*, you must repent and turn away from sin and idolatry so that you might grow in the grace of Jesus Christ *(Revelation 2:5)*.

If God asks you to do a shocking assignment, do it! He knows the plan, purpose, and result of your obedience.

JOEL 2:18

¹⁸ Then the LORD will be zealous for His land, and pity His people.

In the previous verses, the prophet urged the people to blow the trumpet in Zion. But this time, it was a call to a sacred assembly and to consecrate a fast. God's people needed to come together and recommit themselves to Him. In Verse 18, He let us know He stands ready to forgive and bless us, if we repent (change wholeheartedly).

Without a changed people, the world cannot be changed.

Changed people change the world.

AMOS 2:1,8

¹ Thus says the LORD: "For three transgressions of Moab and for four, I will not turn away its punishment, because he burned the bones of the king of Edom to lime."

⁸ They lie down by every altar on clothes taken in pledge, and drink the wine of the condemned in the house of their god.

Burning a dead person's bones was not only despicable, but also considered as an act of desecration. God declared that the poor be afforded the same privileges and care as the rest of society. Amos used hyperbole to demonstrate how the rich seriously distorted the poor, to the point of desiring the dust on their heads. In addition to the sin of greed, there were other injustices such as sexual sins and the cruelty of not returning clothes to the poor so they could keep warm at night.

To further add to the understanding of the message of Amos is to see the exposition of how God despises crimes against humanity, indifference toward people, abusers and cheaters of the poor, and those blinded by false confidence in their special status before God.

Repentance is the key to restoration.

OBADIAH 1:1,8

[1] The vision of Obadiah, thus says the Lord GOD concerning Edom (We have heard a report from the LORD, and a messenger has been sent among the nations, saying, "Arise and let us rise up against her for battle")

[8] "Will I not in that day," says the LORD, "Even destroy the wise men from Edom, and understanding from the mountains of Esau?"

Edom, your day is coming, for the sin of taking delight in the downfall of family. The nation of Edom took full advantage of Judah's humiliation, thus, mocking it when it fell. God noted their cruelty and eventually made them account for it.

In our own lives, we at times, feel that no one notices how we are being treated by people or that there are those who seek to harm us. In many cases, that may very well be the case. It can become difficult to deal with the cruelty, the slight, disparaging, and cutting remarks, the gossip, and the exploitation. All of those things can affect us while we are weak and vulnerable or even contribute to the breakdown of our self-esteem.

But, God loves us and misses nothing that is going on with the just and unjust. His eyes see everything. We can and we must rest our case with Him. Obadiah illustrated the same truth: In time, God will deal justly with those who seek to harm His people.

You may get by, but you don't get away.

JONAH 2:1,8

¹ Then Jonah prayed to the LORD his God from the fish's belly.

⁸ "Those who regard worthless idols forsake their own Mercy..."

Ironically, this is a prayer of thanksgiving from a fish's belly. Jonah described how he felt before the fish swallowed him, believing he had been casted out of God's sight. This is generally the common thought of rebellious people.

Jonah then turned to the Lord for deliverance. Yet, his subsequent behavior did not suggest that his attitude had changed. When repentance is real, people will have the same attitude that God has about their sin: Sin is wrong. Then, they do an about-face and change their attitudes, actions, or deeds.

When you connect with rebellion, you will become an outcast.

MICAH 2:1,8

¹ Woe to those who devise iniquity, and work out evil on their beds! At morning light they practice it, because it is in the power of their hand.

⁸ Lately My people has risen up like an enemy – You pull off the robe with the garment from those who trust you, as they pass by, like men returned from war.

Because the wealthy Israelites were so greedy, they robbed the disenfranchised as if they were the enemy. The scripture depicted them essentially as taking the clothes right off the backs of unsuspecting victims. By rigging the courts in their favor and charging exorbitant taxes, Israel's leaders took away the land of the widows and the fatherless. These abuses made the oppressors targets of God's judgment.

Greedy people can't get enough to consume. They think only about how they can become even richer. God wanted His covenant people to exemplify concern for others instead of exploiting the courts and economic system to their own advantage, as the affluent Israelites were doing. God delivered a stern message to them in *Amos 8:4-7*.

Micah viewed the people as wanting a religion that satisfied their self-indulgence, not one that demanded righteousness and holiness. He was empowered by the Spirit of the Lord with a powerful voice for justice against transgressions and sin. In *Micah 6:8*, the Lord shows how we should walk, love, and behave.

What indulgences do you have that aren't edifying to the Lord?

NAHUM 2:1,8

¹ He who scatters has come up before your face. Man the fort! Watch the road! Strengthen your flanks! Fortify your power mightily.

⁸ Though Nineveh of old was like a pool of water, now they flee away. "Halt! Halt!" they cry; but no one turns back.

The prophet describes the invading army as if he were actually seeing the tumult and terror that would overtake Nineveh. All the details of this scripture drives home divine justice.

After Jonah preached to Nineveh, they repented briefly and God spared judgment. The generation of the repented Assyrians had passed and a new rebellious generation arose to persecute Israel and Judah. Nahum told Assyria that their days were numbered.

Nahum reminds us that God is not absent in the storm. He is our refuge, our strong tower, and our hiding place. And He is good. Although the skies may grow dark, the winds howl, and the dust flies, God never loses sight of His sons and daughters. He sees our plight and He is fully in control.

Be ready at all times.

HABAKKUK 2:1,8

[1] I will stand my watch and set myself on the rampart, and watch to see what He will say to me, and what I will answer when I am corrected.

[8] Because you have plundered many nations, all the remnant of the people shall plunder you, because of men's blood and the violence of the land and the city, and of all who dwell in it.

Known as one of the Minor Prophets, the book of Habakkuk is unique in its style. Rather than speaking to God's people on God's behalf, Habakkuk spoke to God on behalf of the people.

Imagine Habakkuk struggling with understanding God's actions throughout history. He especially did not comprehend his use of an unrighteous nation as the instrument of his justice.

God's answer to Habakkuk's objection was that "the just shall live by faith" (Verse 2:4). It is not that we understand God's ways, but that we trust Him completely. Come what may find strength and sure-footing in God.

Prepare to hear God.

ZEPHANIAH 2:1,8

¹ Gather yourselves together, yes, gather together, O undesirable nation,

⁸ I have heard the reproach of Moab, and the insults of the people of Ammon, with which they have reproached My people.

For years, the people of Judah had been wandering in a fog of idolatry, materialism, and complacency. The tendency for humans to do only what is necessary to avoid bad consequences is complacency. In Zephaniah's day, many said in their hearts that the Lord will not do good, nor will he do evil. The deception of sin leads people to believe they will face no accounting. But, a holy God cannot and will not ignore a laxed spirit.

I implore you to invoke the power of *Psalm 139:23-24* and pray: Search me, O God, and know my heart…and see if there is any wicked way in me, and lead me in the way everlasting.

Squash complacency.

HAGGAI 2:1,8

¹ In the seventh month, on the twenty-first of the month, the word of the LORD came by Haggai, the prophet, saying:

⁸ 'The silver is Mine, and the gold is Mine,' says the LORD of hosts.

Haggai challenged the discouraged people to examine the way they were living and to set new priorities that would please God.

Are you ready for the future? Has your temple been torn down? If it has, then rebuild it.

I lost my courage and became discouraged when my husband died. My normal was challenged. New priorities had to be set in my life. Keep in mind: Our priorities, first things first, should be God's business, then ours. God is sovereign over humanity. It is important to balance our faith with works and God will provide us with strength for our labor. Finally, when we submit to God the struggle is lessened, if not eliminated altogether, with blessings abound.

Submit to God. The struggle is over.

ZECHARIAH 2:1,8

¹ Then I raised my eyes and looked, and behold, a man with a measuring line in his hand.

⁸ For thus says the Lord of hosts: "He sent Me after glory, to the nations which plunder you; for he who touches you touches the apple of His eye."

The key principle throughout Zechariah, as it relates to Israel is return: (a) a return from captivity (a spatial return) and (b) a return to the Lord (a spiritual return). God had withdrawn blessings, but was turning again to favor Israel.

Envision a man with a measuring rod—a surveyor using a tool of divine commissioning—intently measuring Jerusalem from wall to wall. God can choose to judge an entire nation or reserve judgment for a select few. However, He can also choose to protect us and preserve us from the enemy, because He sees us as the apple of His eye.

The apple of the eye refers to the pupil, the most vulnerable part of the body. The metaphor functions to express God's deepest feelings for His chosen people (*Deuteronomy 32:10*).

As God's chosen, the mandates are to: restore, rebuild, rededicate, revere, and repent, for the future is at hand.

Return to the Lord.

MALACHI 2:1,8

[1] "And now, O priests, this commandment is for you."

[8] "But you have departed from the way, you have caused many to stumble at the law. You have corrupted the covenant of Levi," says the LORD of hosts.

This was the last prophetic message from God before the close of the Old Testament. His children, who He called kingdom priests, were called to mediate His grace to the nations. Instead, they profaned His name. God's name is His nature and character. He is revealed by His words and in His actions.

Those who claim to belong to Him will proclaim His nature and character in both their worship and behavior. To not do so, is a misrepresentation of His holiness. We don't want to damage or bring disgrace upon the reputation of God because of our inappropriate deeds. There are consequences for such action *(Leviticus 22:1-16)*. Israel was demonstrating these type of behaviors before they were exiled.

God had set the entire tribe of Levi apart. They were assigned responsibility for the maintenance of the sanctuary, its worship, and teaching the law *(Deuteronomy 10:8-9, Leviticus 10:8-11)*. They were told upfront that they would be responsible for any offenses relative to the sanctuary. The priest corrupted the covenant causing many to stumble. As a result, because they failed to follow the commandments of the Lord, their blessings were cursed.

God calls us a royal priesthood, a chosen generation. We must walk circumspectly before the Lord.

Don't corrupt the covenant. It's your lifeline.

MATTHEW 20:18

¹⁸ Behold, we are going up to Jerusalem, and the Son of Man will be betrayed to the chief priests and to the scribes; and they will condemn Him to death.

God himself, in the form of Jesus, ushered in a new kingdom that would totally be against all earthly kingdoms. Matthew's goal was to show Jesus as the Messiah and the fulfillment of Old Testament prophecy rightfully claiming the Messianic mantle in Jerusalem.

Although the journey to Jerusalem for Jesus and His disciples resulted in betrayal and ultimately His death, the fulfillment of prophecy since the beginning of time would lead to peace in the hearts and minds of those who accept Him wholeheartedly. Confusion, often leading to danger and consequences, results when one disbelieves in the power of the risen Savior and King.

With kingdom living, we are subject to endure what Jesus endured, maybe not to those extremes. But with the help of God and accepting the gift of salvation, we too can endure just as Jesus did. He, the Greater One, lives on the inside of us, which makes us more than conquerors. Jesus was resurrected. Accepting, believing in, and following Him will allow us to dwell with Him now and in eternity.

Stay on track with kingdom living.

MARK 2:18

¹⁸ The disciples of John and of the Pharisees were fasting. Then they came and said to Him, "Why do the disciples of John and of the Pharisees fast, but your disciples do not fast?"

Nothing was wrong with the Jews fasting, as long as it supported its true purpose. That purpose was allowing a person to repent and focus more deeply on God. The Pharisees fasted ritualistically, but it wasn't from the heart. They never realized that God cannot be manipulated. He knows our true intentions.

Mark gives us a means to find focus in a fragmented world. The more confused and chaotic our world becomes, that is more of an opportunity for us to encounter, receive, and deliver the Good News of Jesus Christ. He's the only one who can bring focus and clarity to our lives. There is definitely a reward in getting deep with God.

How deep will you go?

LUKE 20:18

18 Whoever falls on that stone will be broken; but on whomever it falls, it will grind him to powder.

In the Parable of the Vineyard owner, Jesus showed that Israel rejected and killed past prophets that were sent to help them. This was also indicative of future actions of betrayal when Jesus would be rejected and killed by the hands of the very people He was sent to help.

Jesus was the rejected stone. In fact, the New Testament often quotes *Psalm 118:22* in connection with the person and ministry of Jesus Christ and refers to Him as the chief cornerstone of God's kingdom (*Acts 4:11; Ephesians 2:20; 1 Peter 2:7-8*).

In time, God will see to it that He is fully honored by all of His creation, even those who opposed and killed Him. It's important to repent while we have time. We have to acknowledge Jesus for who He is and don't sink deeper into rebellion. Because if we do, destruction will await our presence.

Is your foundation the chief cornerstone?

JOHN 20:18

[18] Mary Magdalene came and told the disciples that she had seen the Lord, and that He had spoken these things to her.

After the resurrection, Jesus revealed Himself to Mary Magdalene and gave her an assignment. He told her to go to His brethren with a clear and distinct message that He will be ascending to His Father. When we get a clear and fresh revelation of who Jesus Christ is, our assignment is to go tell somebody about Him.

What is your assignment?

ACTS 20:18

¹⁸ And when they had come to him, he said to them: "You know, from the first day that I came to Asia, in what manner I always lived among you."

The "manner" in which Paul refers to as he delivers a message to a group of believers pertains to him serving the Lord, his persecution, and his ability to not shrink from teaching the ministry of Jesus Christ to the Jews and Greeks, despite opposition. Paul recognized there was a need for repentance. He represented himself in a manner of integrity, despite being around those who did not have a mature, spiritual understanding. He counted his life as expendable, knowing he had to finish the course.

I believe that the mark of a truly faithful teacher of the gospel is one that keeps nothing back. Though unpopular or perhaps personally difficult, a person of such godly integrity will keep in mind the mission of the church. That person will make repentance a part of his or her life, keep the faith, and speak what the Holy Spirit says to speak with boldness.

What manner are you living among the people?

ROMANS 2:18

18 "and know His will, and approve the things that are excellent, being instructed out of the law"

Knowing God's will is not necessarily discerning a specific decision or path for us to take to lead our own lives. It comes with finding revelation in scripture and agreeing to follow His will. Mere possession of the law does not win divine favor.

Paul took a clear, four-pronged approach in this text: (a) doctrine followed by duty, (b) theology followed by practice, (c) understanding followed by application, and (d) believing followed by doing.

Knowing His will can be further explained as what He requires us to do, what He commands, what He prohibits, what He approves, and what He rewards. This value of truth comes from a covenant relationship with God through Jesus Christ.

Is your revelation God's revelation?

---

1 CORINTHIANS 2:1,8

¹And I brethren, when I came to you, did not come with excellence of speech or of wisdom declaring to you the testimony of God.

⁸Which none of the rulers of this age knew; for had they had known, they would not have crucified the Lord of glory.

Paul's mission and purpose in ministry was to declare the Gospel. He presented the cross and proved that God's wisdom was infinite. Spiritual truth and understanding are not of this world and cannot be discerned in the natural realm. Only God can bring revelation to spiritual wisdom, matters, and principles.

The most prominent people in Jesus's day crucified the Lord of glory. This act blatantly illustrated the foolishness of humanity. They took the wisdom of God and still nailed Him to a tree. However, without His rejection, there would have been no acceptance for humanity and we would not be able to walk in the salvation of the Lord.

Let us be careful not to take the wisdom of God and nail it to the cross again.

---

2 CORINTHIANS 2:1,8

¹But I determined this within myself, that I would not come again to you in sorrow.

⁸Therefore I urge you to reaffirm your love to him.

Godly correction is necessary. Depending upon the delivery of the message by the messenger, the one receiving it could become sorrowful. Hurt is always the possibility when redirection and change are necessary. If you're operating in the leading and guidance of the Holy Spirit, the receiver is less likely to reject the message because he or she will agree with the confirmation. Pouring on love in counsel can lead to conviction and change may occur. Being led by the flesh could only lead to destruction and draw the listener further away from God. A condemning, guilt-laden approach could very well drown a person and lead to no change or maybe even a temporary change.

When discipline occurs in church, although it may feel like punishment, the ultimate goal is for redemption to occur. Upon repentance, believers are called to forgive and provide comfort to those who were in error. Using judgment is wise, particularly when you have a believer who is constantly overtaken in a sin. If that person seems to be starting a pattern of repenting and sinning and there's no real change occurring, a conversation is necessary to discern if additional steps of discipline needs to occur.

One of the most severe church discipline is excommunication (*Matthew 18:17; 2 Corinthians 5:5*). A person who has been excommunicated will go through a period of restriction or exclusion (temporary or permanent). The appropriate leadership usually determines the level or nature of this limitation.

Pour on the love of Christ.

GALATIANS 2:1,8

¹ Then after fourteen years I went up again to Jerusalem with Barnabas, and also took Titus with me.

⁸ (For He who worked effectively in Peter for the apostleship to the circumcised also worked effectively in me toward the Gentiles).

It was not uncommon for many to defend the Gospel of Jesus Christ, particularly when it came to the act of circumcision. *Acts 15:2* gives a description of a dispute over circumcision versus uncircumcision as it relates to salvation, which led Paul, Barnabus, and others to go to Jerusalem to seek wisdom from the apostles and elders.

Paul's ministry to the uncircumcised (Gentiles) was not a different gospel from Peter's ministry to the circumcised (Jews). Salvation, uncircumcised or circumcised, is simply accepting Jesus Christ.

Circumcised or saved? That is the question.

EPHESIANS 2:1,8

¹ And you He made alive, who were dead in trespasses and sins

⁸ For by grace you have been saved through faith, and that not of yourselves, it is a gift of God.

Paul drew contrast between the human condition and a new life in Christ. God's lovingkindness and mercy not only makes new life possible, but it enthrones us with Christ. Because Jesus, the Exalted One, following the resurrection, is now seated at the right side of the Father, we who are in Christ have a direct line to the Father (*Ephesians 2:18*) and the devil cannot tap in on that line.

The salvation of men and women is a display of divine grace. Salvation can only be given by God's grace and glory, not through human works and achievements. Nor, is it given by our popularity or who's in our family. It's not given by our pedigree or the kind of car we drive. Our looks do not even play a part.

Salvation is given only through the profession of Jesus Christ, accepting Him as our Lord and Savior, believing that He died for our sins, and as a result, we shall be born again. Simply put, salvation is a gift of God's unmerited favor. When someone gives us a gift, we should cherish it. We can cherish our gift of salvation through faith, obedience, and trusting the Lord.

Salvation is God's divine favor for all of history to see.

PHILIPPIANS 2:18

^{18} For the same reason you also be glad and rejoice with me.

The sacrificial system was evident throughout the Old Testament. In *Numbers 15:5*, the Lord instructed Moses to tell the children of Israel to make a sacrifice or burnt offering of grain and drink. He was very specific about the kind and the measurements of those offerings.

However, the Lord didn't require those kind of offerings in Philippians. Paul considered himself to be a drink offering. He was a vessel used to pour out the Good News of Jesus Christ onto the people.

The Lord called us to be living sacrifices. Jesus is the perfect example for us to follow. He was humble, thus making himself of no reputation, as He did the work of the Lord. Although we live in this world, we are not called to conform to its ways, but to be sober-minded as we seek to transform and renew our own minds, which in turn, will transform the world into the ways of the Lord as we walk in humility (*Romans 12:1-3*).

What a way to rejoice! If you ever need to rekindle and reflect on the joy of the Lord, *Ephesians 2:8* is a great reminder. Just thinking about the gift of salvation is cause for celebration.

Let's stay humble.

COLOSSIANS 2:18

^{18} Let no one cheat you of your reward, taking delight in false humility and worship of angels, intruding into those things which he has not seen, vainly puffed up by his fleshly mind.

When you hear the word cheat, do you automatically think about an athletic competition where rules are being violated? Oftentimes, in the sports arena, cheating can lead to penalties, such as fines, ejection, jail time, or being barred from future competitions.

Unfortunately, there are those who cheat in the spiritual arenas. There are teachers who impose false spiritual disciplines on their audience for their own selfish ambitions. If we're not rooted and grounded in God's Word, or spending time with Him and seeking His face, we can easily be deceived with the many voices of man. The way to tell the difference between the authentic and counterfeit spiritual leaders is with discernment. Discernment is a gift that comes with yielding to the Holy Spirit.

I believe the discernment is even more activated, when one remains humble. Because the Lord calls us to be humble (*Philippians 2:3-11*), to not do so means we are being disobedient. There are those who operate in false humility. These individuals are carnal with vainly puffed-up, egotistical delusions, thinking more highly of themselves than they ought to. A truly humble-minded person will never have to make an announcement telling another person he or she is humble. It will be evident in their character traits, so study their actions.

We don't want to disqualify ourselves from the rewards that God has for us on earth and in heaven. So take time to repent, refocus, and walk in humility.

Get out of your carnal mind.

---

1 THESSALONIANS 2:18

¹⁸ Therefore we wanted to come to you—even I, Paul, time and again—but Satan hindered us.

Think about the military when armies put barriers or roadblocks to impede the enemy's forces. When this happens, they are essentially being hindered from completing their mission. In many cases, when obstacles are placed in our way, we are faced with the decision of what to do. Should we go forth or abort the mission and instructions of Christ? Paul's time in Thessalonica was cut short because of the fast rising tide of persecution. He had a deep desire to return to Thessalonica, but Satan hindered him (*Roman 1:13; Romans 15:22*).

Satan takes extreme measures in an attempt to prevent people from doing God's will. We can combat Satan's barriers with: (a) the name of Jesus, (b) the Word of God, (c) the blood of Jesus, (d) the anointing, and (e) the knowledge that we have power and authority in Christ.

If there is fire in our hearts for Jesus, then sparks of truth declaring the Word of the Lord will spew out of our mouths with confidence, boldness, and assurance.

Desiring God, but hindered by Satan.

2 THESSALONIANS 2:1,8

¹ Now, brethren, concerning the coming of our Lord Jesus Christ and our gathering together to Him, we ask you,

⁸ And then the lawless one will be revealed, whom the Lord will consume with the breath of His mouth and destroy with the brightness of His coming.

The believers will be gathered together at the 'Rapture.' *Daniel 12:2-3, Mathew 13:41, 50, Mathew 25:41, John 3:36, Romans 1:18, 21, 25,* and *Hebrews 9:27-28* explain the judgment process, the wrath of God, along with the catastrophic events that must precede the rapture of the Church.

So, what can we expect at the end of the age? The Lord told us in the Word what will occur throughout the Old and New Testaments. First, the truth will be rejected. We know that the Lord has an appointed time for everything. In *2 Thessalonians 2:6-7,* the restraint that was put on the man of sin (the antichrist or son of perdition) will be removed. This antichrist will be revealed with all power, signs, and wonders much like what Jesus performed, but coupled with an unrighteous deception. There will be many who will fall prey to this deception and abandon the truth that they once believed. However, this deceiver of lawlessness will be consumed and destroyed at the coming of the Lord.

Now is the time to decide where we want to spend eternity. Do we want to practice lawlessness and risk the chance of burning in the lake of fire, or do we want to go to heaven where there is peace forevermore?

Jesus is contagious! Once you taste His goodness and mercy, you will not be able to get enough of Him.

---

1 TIMOTHY 2:1,8

¹ Therefore I exhort first of all that supplications, prayers, intercessions, and giving of thanks be made for all men.

⁸ I desire therefore that the men pray everywhere, lifting up holy hands, without wrath and doubting.

Paul instructs us on how to pray: (a) supplication (an urgent request based on a need), (b) intercession (involves speaking to God on behalf of others), and (c) a prayer of thanksgiving.

It was a traditional practice for Jewish men to assume the prayer posture of praying with their arms lifted up and their hands open *(Psalm 134:2)*. Holy hands represent an innocent or blameless life, untarnished by anger or interpersonal conflict *(Psalm 66:18)*.

We want the Lord to hear us, so we should have something more than just a prayer posture. So, if you're unable to get down on your knees or lift your hands due to physical limitations, don't limit your worship unto the Lord. If your vocal box isn't allowing you to speak through your mouth, the Lord hears your words from your heart. Worship, praise, and obedience will reach the heart of God.

Prayer is a channel to God.

---

2 TIMOTHY 2:1,8

¹ You therefore, my son, be strong in the grace that is in Christ Jesus.

⁸ Remember that Jesus Christ, of the seed of David, was raised from the dead according to my gospel.

This text is a reminder that we are to overcome and renew our commitment to Christ. The words are like oil for our souls and our directed paths. The seed of David is a reminder of the Messianic role of Jesus. He was the one the Lord sent to redeem the times. Christ Jesus has overcome the world for us. He encourages us to remain steadfast because the grace that He provides for us will give us strength in our weakness, clarity in dark places, and make our crooked paths straight *(Isaiah 45:2)*.

Be strong. We have a powerful backing.

TITUS 2:1,8

¹ But as for you, speak the things which are proper for sound doctrine.

⁸ Sound speech that cannot be condemned, that one who is an opponent may be ashamed, having nothing evil to say to you.

It is important to walk circumspectly and speak only the oracles of God with sobriety and soundness. Titus taught the people to live in a way that would affirm, rather than deny their claim to know God. To be 'sound' pertains to the desired result of gospel living—the truths, attitudes, and actions of our everyday living. We are to be effective witnesses to unbelievers and not blasphemers or slanderers. The way we live our lives should serve as a reminder, as demonstrated by our character, that we have a responsibility to represent the Gospel to the fullest.

Don't let your deeds profane the name of God.

PHILEMON 1:8

⁸ Therefore, though I might be very bold in Christ to command you what is fitting

When Paul was serving a two-year house arrest in Rome, he was allowed to receive visitors. Philemon was one of his visitors. He was an affluent Christian leader in the Colossian Church. He became saved under Paul's ministry. He owned at least one slave, a man named Onesimus. Onesimus stole money from Philemon and ran away. Later, Onesimus met Paul in Rome and became a Christian.

Paul knew Onesimus had broken Roman law and defrauded his master. As a Christian, Paul knew those matters had to be dealt with. Paul decided to send Onesimus back to Philemon in Colossae with Tychicus, who was to deliver an epistle to the Colossians. He also sent a personal letter to Philemon urging him to forgive Onesimus and welcome him back to service as a brother in Christ.

Philemon provided valuable insight into the early church's relationship and the institution of slavery. Slavery was widespread, constituting close to one-third of the population. In Paul's day, slavery equated to free labor. Slaves could be in any profession—doctors, musicians, teachers, artists, librarians, or accountants. Slaves could fill almost all jobs.

Slaves were not legally considered as people, but they were the tools of their masters. As such, they could be bought, sold, inherited, exchanged, or seized in order to pay for their masters' debts. While they were recognized as persons under the law, the Romans granted trials to slaves who were accused of crimes.

Rather than directly attacking slavery or condemning the institution as being wrong, the perils and evils of the institution were surmised by changing the hearts of the slaves and their masters. By stressing the spiritual equality of master and slave (*Philemon 1:16; Galatians 3:28; Ephesians 6:9; Colossians 4:1; I Timothy 6:1-2*), the Bible did away with spiritual abuses. The rich theological theme that dominates the letter is forgiveness. Without even using the word forgiveness, it is evident that this is what Paul's instruction—the heart of the gospel is about.

God is our Master.

HEBREWS 2:1,8

¹ Therefore we must give the more earnest heed to the things we have heard, lest we drift away.

⁸ You have put all things in subjection under his feet. For in that He put all in subjection under him, He left nothing that is not put under him. But now we do not yet see all things put under him.

Diligently apply your mind and pay detailed attention to the messages of Christ. If we don't take the Word of God seriously, we are subject to drifting away from the truth like a sailing vessel that has broken free of its moorings.

When we drift away from the covering of the Word, we jeopardize our dominion and may fall short of our ability to put all things—mindsets, habits, or patterns in proper perspective as it relates to God. The original plan, as illustrated in *Genesis 1:28*, was that man would subdue and rule the creatures in the land. However, with the actions of Adam and Eve, turmoil came as a result *(Genesis 3:16-19)*. Because of the sacrifices of Jesus, God will restore humanity to its intended place of authority *(Psalm 8:6)*.

Pay attention to the Gospel or drift away.

JAMES 2:1,8

¹ My brethren, do not hold the faith of our Lord Jesus Christ, the Lord of glory, with partiality.

⁸ If you really fulfill the royal law according to the Scripture, "You shall love your neighbor as yourself," you do well.

Whenever James uses the words 'my brethren,' it is to point out something that we all need to change in our lives. He denounced all forms of prejudice, snobbishness, and lack of respect for persons. Some people believe the blessings of God are only bestowed upon the wealthy. But, that's not true. God has sensitivity towards the poor. He is not in the business of partiality, showing favoritism only towards the well-to-do. In fact, God doesn't show favoritism at all, and He forbids us from playing favorites also. Such conduct dishonors the Lord (*Deuteronomy 1:17*). With the same measure of grace we expect to receive, we should offer that to our neighbors as well.

What do you need to change?

1 PETER 2:1,8

¹ Therefore, laying aside all malice, all deceit, hypocrisy, envy, and all evil speaking.

⁸ and "A stone of stumbling and a rock of offense." They stumble, being disobedient to the word, to which they also were appointed.

Growth is essential in the pursuit of holiness. Before we can grow, we must first be planted in the soil of love, thus removing the weeds of sin (malice, deceit, envy, and evil speaking) that stagnate our growth. Another element of growth is having a desire for God's Word, which will cause us to read, study, and meditate on it daily.

A spiritually thirsty Christian is a strong Christian. God's Word is the perfect nourishment for a life of faith. Think of ourselves as spiritual buildings. We can construct each layer of the building with stones of holiness, stones of faithfulness, stones of belief, and stones of righteousness. That can only be accomplished if we allow the Holy Spirit to dwell within us.

The Christian faith and the entire church are built on Jesus. People will see Jesus either as: (a) one who offends their personal freedom (a stone of stumbling) or as (b) one who frees them of sin and is worthy of their worship and obedience (the chief cornerstone). Truth offends those who do not want to hear it. However, to the growing believer, it is life.

Remove the weeds for growth.

2 PETER 2:18

¹⁸ For when they speak great swelling words of emptiness, they allure through the lusts of the flesh, through lewdness, the ones who have actually escaped from those who live in error.

There are predators on the prowl. They live by lust and are addicted to filthiness. They despise authority, preferring to indulge in vain conceit and slandering others. They make their own rules and govern themselves as kings. They lurk around the corners of our minds and in our hearts trying to get us to turn from the holy hands of God. Predators of this nature have left the main road of God. They are now on a path with no direction.

When we step out of the will of God, we all are subjected to become predators in our own lives or others, disturbing the peace that God promised to provide to us if we kept our minds stayed on Him. We don't want to be dried up fountains of missed opportunities to seek the glory of the Lord. We certainly don't want to create scattered storms throughout our lives and others. This will only cause us to head towards the black hole, which is Hell. Defiance makes us more susceptible to being seduced by the tricks of the enemy. Escape now if you're in the midst of a sin-filled life. Allow God to be your spiritual compass, leading you back to the path of righteousness.

The main road is God. Seek His direction for your life.

1 JOHN 2:18

18 Little children, it is the last hour; and as you have heard that the Antichrist is coming, even now many antichrists have come, by which we know that it is the last hour.

John knew that we will live in the last hour—meaning that the current time foreshadowed the final period of history before Christ returns. The Antichrist will arise claiming to be God, but in reality, will actually be opposing God and leading people astray.

Many only consider the Antichrist as the finality of this world and think we won't see his existence until then. I have to let you know that this counterfeit spirit is already residing in the earth. It has presented itself in those who are deceiving God's people through false teaching.

Know the Lord in His ways, voice, and commandments, so that you will not fall victim to the Antichrist.

---

2 JOHN 1:8

⁸Look to yourselves, that we do not lose those things that we worked for, but that we may receive a full reward.

Many deceivers stand ready to mislead and disrupt congregations. They sow seeds of confusion—getting people not to acknowledge or operating in the full divinity of Jesus. Any type of stagnancy or rebellion can make a congregation more susceptible to the wiles, schemes, and tactics of the devil.

It is a dangerous thing to become lethargic in our Christian living or take God's favor for granted. Imagine living and doing the "works" of God diligently for years, only for the Lord to tell us He never knew us at judgment time *(Luke 13:27)*. It is important to make sure the "works" we're doing are what God instructed and purposed us to do.

Sometimes, we can become entangled in busy work that God never intended for us that takes our focus off Him *(Luke 10:38-41)*. You can become so skilled in an area or task, that you can do it effortlessly. But, that doesn't mean that it is done with the anointing of Christ.

Some may take on several tasks in the church to make themselves appear holy, but in reality, they may not even have a relationship with Christ. They are pretending and perhaps hoping they can buy their way into the blessings of Christ or even into heaven. We must be careful to check our motives by asking ourselves, "Am I doing this assignment for the glory of: (a) God, (b) man, or (c) myself?" I can assure you, if you're doing it for any purpose other than the Lord, you can find yourself in idolatry quickly.

Love and obedience are critical.
2 John 1:5-6

---

3 JOHN 1:2,8

² Beloved, I pray that you may prosper in all things and be in health, just as your soul prospers.

⁸ We therefore ought to receive such, that we may become fellow workers for the truth.

If we follow the Lord and keep the faith, we can expect to prosper in every area of our lives—physically, spiritually, mentally, and financially. In order to prosper, we must adhere to the truth. When we commit ourselves to God's truths and communicate His love, we will experience His grace, mercy, and peace. We should count it as a privilege of our Christian identity to be workers of truth.

Vigor + Truth = Rewards

JUDE 1:1,18

¹ ...To those who are called, sanctified by God the Father, and preserved in Jesus Christ

¹⁸ How they told you there would be mockers in the last time who would walk according to their own ungodly lusts.

Jude urged us to remember that the 'called' are those who respond in faith, salvation, sanctification, and preservation of the Word. Let us not forget there are those who seek to cause divisions. They don't have God's spirit. They are pretenders, manipulators, and deceivers who walk according to their own lusts—grumbling, complaining, and maintaining swelling words of flattery—to gain advantage over others.

We have to contend for our faith in God for our family and in life's situations, because our faith will be tried. Intruders will come in every area of our life. These intruders, which are referred to as principalities (*Ephesians 6:12*), will manifest themselves in people. Often, they are the people we are closest to or the ones who are in authority. These wicked powers will create chaos in our marriage, wreak havoc on our job, and cause us to lose focus, hope, and belief in Christ. The whole purpose is to cause us to doubt and retreat from the Lord.

In order to maintain the foundation and covering of Christ, we have to set our affections on things above *(Colossians 3:2)*.

―――――――――――――――――――――

Status check: Where are you in God?

―――――――――――――――――――――

REVELATION 20:1,8

¹ Then I saw an angel coming down from heaven, having the key to the bottomless pit and a great chain in his hand.

⁸ And will go out to deceive the nations which are in the four corners of the earth, Gog, and Magog, to gather them together to battle, whose number is as the sand of the sea.

This vision was recorded to inform us that following His return to earth, the Lord Jesus will deal with Satan.

Let's focus on the rapture when the saints will be caught up with the Lord. The tribulation will begin on earth. In his vision, John sees Christ coming to earth after the tribulation. The heavenly armies, who will be clothed in white fine linen, will accompany Christ *(Revelation 19:4; Revelation 19:7-8)*.

At the rapture, Christ will come for His bride (the church), celebrate the marriage feast with her in heaven during the tribulation, and return with her to earth at His second coming. The saints of God, who return with Him for the battle of Armageddon, will rule from the New Jerusalem, helping to oversee a thousand years of peace and righteousness on earth, while Satan is bound. Everyone entering the Millennial Kingdom will be a believer.

Satan will be released after a thousand years and it will show two things: (1) He has not changed and (2) The heart of man is desperately wicked. Satan will recruit an army to attack Jerusalem, the abode of Christ. People will volunteer for the army to attack the saints under the leadership of Gog and Magog.

God wins and Christ triumphs, of course. As righteousness prevails, Satan loses; and sorrow, sickness, and death will disappear. A new heaven and new earth will emerge.

Regardless of what happens in this life—no matter how depressing the world news becomes or how difficult or dark the season we endure—it is better to have a life in Christ. When the heartache of this present world weighs heavily on us, we only have to look up and look ahead at His radiance in anticipation for a joyous beginning of a new story. Our story with the Lord will never end in eternity. We win! Worthy is the Lamb who was sacrificed for our sins *(Revelation 5:12).*

There's too much world in the church, and not enough church in the world.

EPILOGUE

My prayer is that whoever reads this book espouses it upon hearing the Spirit of the Lord Jesus Christ. Embrace it as a Ready Word, a present help in trouble, in triumph, in peace, in joy, and even in time to just love on God. My perspective is to search for revelation that leads to a lighted pathway every time I look into the book. That is my desire for you as well. After all, the entire Bible is the book of life revealed with a pathway of light to find ourselves.

This book can be treated as a devotional or a go-to for life's situations. As a counselor, I can't always rely on my words, but I can rely on God's wisdom.

ABOUT THE AUTHOR

Dr. Gloria Gilmore Watkins, born and raised in Columbia, SC, graduated from CA Johnson High School. She received a Bachelor's degree from the University of South Carolina and attended graduate classes at Columbia International University and Liberty University.

Dr. Watkins holds a Doctorate in Christian Counseling from Central Christian University of SC. She also attended the Sarasota Academy of Christian Counseling, which led to her being licensed under the National Association of Christian Counselors (NACC).

Dr. Watkins is currently employed as Dean of the Christian Counseling Department at Central Christian University of SC.

She notes that her greatest achievement was the day she received Jesus as her personal Savior.

She enjoys reading, crossword puzzles, and watching God's glory be manifested every time the sun rises and sets.